ENGLISH CAMEO GLASS

IN

THE CORNING MUSEUM OF GLASS

DAVID WHITEHOUSE

THE CORNING MUSEUM OF GLASS
CORNING, NEW YORK

Cover: *Moorish Bathers*. England, Amblecote,
Thomas Webb & Sons, carved and engraved by
George Woodall, 1898. D. 46.3 cm. The
Corning Museum of Glass (92.2.10, bequest of
Mrs. Leonard S. Rakow).

Copyright © 1994
The Corning Museum of Glass
Corning, New York 14830-2253

Editor: John H. Martin
Photography: Nicholas L. Williams

Design and Typography: Graphic Solutions,
Corning, New York
Printing: Upstate Litho, Rochester, New York

Standard Book Number 0-87290-134-3
Library of Congress Catalog Card Number
94-071702

FRONTISPIECE. *The Great Dish.*

CONTENTS

FIG. 1. The Portland Vase.

THIS SHORT BOOK has two objectives: to celebrate the achievements of 19th-century English cameo glass makers and to focus attention on the outstanding examples of their work in the collection of The Corning Museum of Glass.

Cameos are objects with two or more layers of different colors. The outer layer or layers are partly removed to create relief decoration on a background of contrasting color. Shading is produced by thinning the carved layer, an effect fully exploited by George Woodall in the *Moorish Bathers* (cover and Fig. 45). Highlights occur in the places where the upper layer is thickest, as in the portraits on John Northwood's Shakespeare, Newton, and Flaxman *tazza*s (Fig. 17).

The first cameo glass vessels were made by the Romans between about 25 B.C. and A.D. 50. A handful of vessels were produced by Roman glassworkers in the fourth century A.D., rather more were made by Islamic craftsmen between the ninth and 11th centuries, and Chinese glass cutters in and after the 18th century made more cameo glasses than all their predecessors combined. Nevertheless, cameo glass was comparatively rare until the late 19th century, when glassmakers in the Stourbridge area of central England produced tens of thousands of objects for consumption at home and abroad.

The most famous Roman cameo glass is the Portland Vase, which is decorated with scenes that may represent the fall of Troy and the rise of imperial Rome. The vase was discovered in Italy in the late 16th century. It was brought to England in 1783, and the following year it was acquired by the dowager duchess of Portland. Although it was placed in the British Museum in 1810, the vase remained the property of the dukes of Portland until 1945, when the museum purchased it. Immediately after its arrival in England, the vase became an icon of the neo-classical style, and the English master potter Josiah Wedgwood invested years of effort in producing accurate ceramic replicas. These replicas and the presence of the original in the British Museum virtually guaranteed the fame of the Portland Vase in Britain. In 1818, two Birmingham glass-

makers tried unsuccessfully to make a replica of it, and in the 1820s and 1830s several silver versions were made by the London firm of Rundle, Bridge, and Rundell.

In the early 19th century—possibly as early as 1804—glassmakers in Bohemia began to "case," or cover, colorless glass with a layer of colored glass that was then cut through to reveal the underlay, and by 1836, they were making vessels with two or more different overlays. By the 1840s, the products of Bohemian factories were attracting much attention in Britain and the United States. They stimulated a lively reaction. The English firm of W. H., B. & J. Richardson exhibited blue, green, and red cased glass at the Manchester Exhibition in 1845–1846, and the April 1846 issue of the British *Art-Union* magazine noted that

> Messrs. Richardson are directing considerable attention to the improvement of coloured glasses; in this art we yet lag behind our neighbours; chemistry has at present done little for this country; these gentlemen have, however, already made great advances in rivaling the productions of Bohemia; and we have little doubt that a few years hence, we shall see at least equal the best of the imported articles; their specimens of opal glass are remarkably successful; and of cutting, engraving, and polishing, they supply examples second to none that have ever been produced in this country.[1]

At about this time, the sensational breaking of the Portland Vase renewed public awareness of this masterpiece of ancient cameo glass. (The vase was on loan to the British Museum, where, in 1845, a visitor deliberately smashed it.) A Richardson design book of about 1845–1850 shows, among other classical themes intended to be transfer-printed on glass, the scenes on the sides and base of the vase.

In short, by the middle of the 19th century, glassmakers in England and on the Continent possessed the technical skill required to produce glasses with overlays, and in England there was a fascination with the Portland Vase. Indeed,

FIG. 2. Josiah Wedgwood's replica of the Portland Vase.

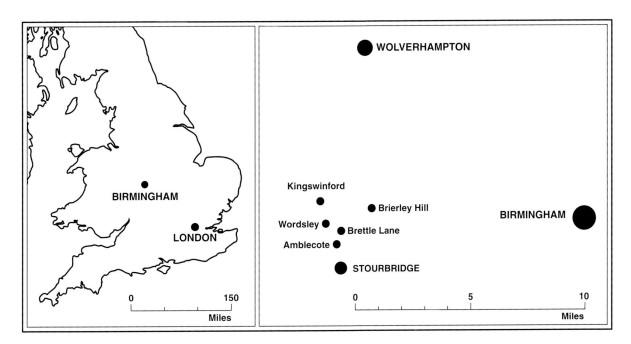

FIG. 3. The Stourbridge area.

Roman cameo glasses—notably, the Portland Vase—were the direct inspiration of the English cameo glass revival.

The manufacture of cameo glass reached its greatest height in England and France in the second half of the 19th century. In England, George Woodall (1850–1925) supervised the carving of elaborate scenes that display his exceptional technical skill. In France, Emile Gallé (1846–1904) directed a manufactory that produced extraordinary glasses carved and engraved from blanks with overlays in the form of numerous trails, blobs, and pads of colored glass. These glasses expressed in visual terms the poetic images of their creator.

English cameo glasses were highly prized, and examples were exhibited regularly at international trade fairs. Joseph Locke's replica of the Portland Vase (Fig. 21) won a silver medal at the Paris world's fair of 1878; the Woodall Team's *The Great Dish*, *The Great Tazza*, and a spectacular lamp base (frontispiece, Fig. 28, and Fig. 48) were exhibited in Paris in 1889; and one of

George Woodall's *Aphrodite* plaques (Fig. 35) was shown at the World's Columbian Exposition in Chicago in 1893.

Despite their success, the glasses of Woodall and his contemporaries are not to everyone's taste. Critics find them cold and "academic"— comparable, perhaps, with the canvases of successful Victorian painters such as Lord Leighton and Sir Lawrence Alma-Tadema. Admirers, on the other hand, point to their technical mastery and the sensitive treatment of figures, as in Woodall's portraits of Dr. and Mrs. Cadman (Fig. 36).

The center of the English cameo glass industry was Stourbridge, a city on the edge of the "Black Country." This region, one of the cradles of the Industrial Revolution, derived its popular name from the soot emitted by the smokestacks of its foundries and factories. In 1975, Michael Braby described the Black Country as "a criss-cross of canals, mineral railways, slag heaps and other relics of the Industrial Revolution."[2]

Glass had been produced in the Stourbridge

area since the 17th century. In 1615, the use of wood for firing furnaces was made illegal in England, and glassmakers switched to coal. This was readily available in the Black Country; indeed, glassmakers at Greensforge, near Stourbridge, were already using it. Soon they were joined by immigrant glassmakers from Lorraine, and by 1696 Stourbridge was the home of 17 of the 88 glasshouses in England and Wales recorded by John Houghton.

In 1845, the British government repealed the Glass Excise Act, which had imposed taxes on raw materials and required glassmakers to pay an annual license fee and to keep detailed records of their activities. Freed from these obligations, which discouraged research and development, glassmaking became a highly competitive industry. The Stourbridge glassmakers rose to the occasion, quickly establishing an international reputation for the quality of their tableware.

The acknowledged leader of the industry was Benjamin Richardson (1802–1887). Ben (as he was known) entered the glass industry in 1825, when he joined the Wordsley Flint Glass Works. In 1829, Ben, his brother William Haden Richardson, and Thomas Webb established a new factory, Richardson and Webb. Webb left this company in 1836, and the Richardsons, with their brother Jonathan, founded W. H., B. & J. Richardson. The firm became famous, winning gold or silver medals from the Society of Arts of London in 1847, 1848, and 1849, and a prize medal at the Great Exhibition of 1851. This, however, did not save the owners from bankruptcy in 1852, although the company was refounded and soon resumed its leading role among Stourbridge glass factories.

One of the secrets of Ben Richardson's success was his ability to identify and hire outstanding craftsmen. These included Philip Pargeter, who became the proprietor of the Red House Glass Works; John Northwood, the future director of design at Stevens & Williams; Joseph Locke, who later enjoyed a highly successful career at the New England Glass Company in East Cambridge, Massachusetts; and George Woodall, the greatest of all the English cameo glass artists. The Richardsons also recruited the French medalist and gem engraver Alphonse Lechevrel to teach their decorators the art of cameo glass engraving.

The vogue for cameo glass was short-lived. Cameo glass attracted attention and began to win prizes in the 1870s, and it was still popular in the early 1900s. "No more noble ornament can be conceived in a room than a fine well-designed and artistically executed cameo glass," wrote Owen Gibbons in *The Pottery Gazette* on January 1, 1908. Four years later, however, George Woodall reported that the market for it had been ruined by inexpensive enameled imitations.

The Corning Museum of Glass celebrated English cameo glass in 1963, when it mounted an exhibition drawn from the collection of Mr. and Mrs. Albert C. Revi of Dallas, Texas. In 1982, the Museum organized a much larger exhibition of cameo glass. Although the objects were made at various times between the first century B.C. and the present, three-quarters of them were English. In recent years, thanks in particular to the munificence of the late Dr. and Mrs. Leonard S. Rakow, the Museum has expanded its holdings of English cameo glass and related materials, with the result that the collection is one of the finest in the world.

Almost all of the objects, photographs, and drawings in this book are in The Corning Museum of Glass or its Rakow Library. Some of them were formerly in the Revi Collection. A larger number, including many of the most important pieces, were in the collection of Dr. and Mrs. Rakow. The Rakows were among the Museum's greatest benefactors, and this book pays homage to their generosity.

David Whitehouse
Director
The Corning Museum of Glass

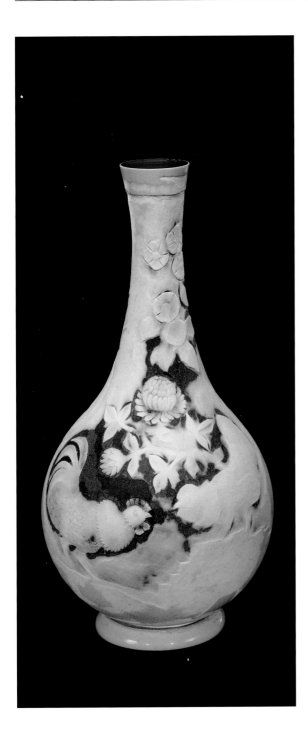

FIG. 4. Vase (unfinished) carved by Joshua Hodgetts.

CAMEO GLASSES are made in two stages. First, the undecorated "blank" with at least two layers of different colors must be prepared; then, after the blank has been gradually cooled to eliminate stresses in the glass, it must be decorated.

Unlike Roman cameo glasses, which were carved, ground, and polished, later 19th-century examples were also treated with acid. The use of hydrofluoric acid to etch glass seems to have been discovered by Carl Wilhelm Scheele in Sweden in 1771. However, despite repeated experiments with hydrofluoric acid on glass, Scheele's discovery was not applied industrially until the early 1850s. In Stourbridge, Benjamin Richardson pioneered the industrial application of acid etching, and in 1857 he patented a method of etching through cased glass.

The introduction of acid etching changed the way in which cameo glasses were finished. Now they were decorated in as many as five stages. In the first stage, the decorator took the blank prepared by the glassmaker and dulled the surface by immersing it in a solution of potassium fluoride. This enabled the artist to draw the design on the surface. Some decorators, including John Northwood, worked from carefully prepared drawings, while others, such as George Woodall, drew the design directly on the blank. The drawing shown in Fig. 5 is the *only* preliminary drawing by Woodall that is known to exist. The second stage was to paint parts of the design with a varnish consisting mainly of beeswax, which, when it hardened, resisted the attack of hydrofluoric acid. In the third stage, the entire object was immersed in hydrofluoric acid so that the unwanted parts of the overlay could be removed by etching. Stage four began with trimming and smoothing the results of the immersion in acid. The details were then carved with gravers of carefully tempered steel mounted in wooden holders, and with copper wheels fed with a mixture of oil and emery. In the final stage, the craftsman polished the object with emery cloth and sticks, as well as with wooden and cork wheels.

The plaque illustrated opposite, which depicts Antony's first meeting with Cleopatra, was abandoned long before completion. It shows clearly how a cameo glass blank was decorated. The white overlay was partly coated with a "resist," which withstood the corrosive effect of the hydrofluoric acid. The first application of acid etched the outline of the scene. Further details were added by repeated applications, and removal, of the resist and the acid.

John Northwood II described the process and its attendant hardship as follows:

> For bowls, plates, dishes and other articles, we made a stubby shaped handle out of wood and pitched it to the bottom of the article. We had to keep removing the scum formed on the glass where acid was acting to prevent it eating down in an uneven way. To do this we had sticks of wood with a pad of cotton wool tied on the end which we called a "mop." The operation was to stand over the vat and whilst moving the article in the acid with one hand, we rubbed the mop over the surface of the glass with the other. So you see we could not get very far away from the fumes. It was always an unpleasant job and nobody wanted it.[3]

The plaque was etched at least six times. After repeatedly bathing the blank in acid, the decorator began his task of engraving the ornament, but almost immediately a bubble was dis-

FIG. 5. *Cleopatra,* by George Woodall.

covered at the upper left. The plaque was abandoned, but it is prized today because it shows the extent to which Victorian cameo glasses were etched before they reached the hands of the carver.

The problem of hidden bubbles was solved in 1895, when Wilhelm Conrad Röntgen discovered X-rays. Soon George and Thomas Woodall were using X-rays to examine blanks prepared for carving, thereby avoiding lost time due to the late discovery of flaws. The Woodalls' swift application of radiography illustrates very well the way in which Stourbridge glassmakers responded to advances in technology.

After the acid etching had been completed, the object was handed to the carver, who finished it with hand tools and engraving wheels, and by grinding and polishing. James M. O'Fallon, a member of the Woodall Team employed at Thomas Webb & Sons (see page 33), described the finishing process as follows:

> During [hand] work the article was laid on a pad of ample size, filled with soft but firm material such as bran. The tool was held in the right hand by the thumb and first two fingers, while the thumb on the left hand was held and pressed against the side of the tool to form a fulcrum as it were during the act of carving. If heavy or continuous work was being done, a thumb-stall of leather was worn on the end of the left thumb to prevent soreness.[4]

FIG. 6. *Antony and Cleopatra.*

FIG. 7. *The Attack* (unfinished), carved by
Thomas and George Woodall, about 1899.

FIG. 8. *The Attack* at an early stage of carving.

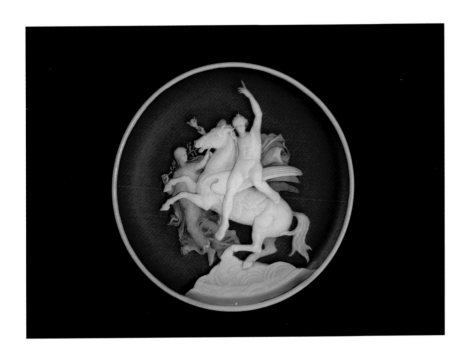

FIG. 9. *The Immortality of the Arts*, carved by Frederick Carder.

FIG. 10. Graver.

The hand tools were very simple. According to John Northwood II, his father designed his own: they "were simply wooden handles of the shape of thick lead-pencils with finely tempered silver steel rods driven through them and ground at their working end to a tapered three-cornered point." The tools used by Frederick Carder (1863–1963) to carve the unfinished plaque in Fig. 9 were essentially the same. The graver illustrated in Fig. 10 consists of a pointed steel rod set in a brass tube. The illustration below shows the hands of Frederick Carder in 1951, posed above his unfinished cameo glass plaque of 1887.

FIG. 11. Frederick Carder's hands, demonstrating how he carved *The Immortality of the Arts* using the graver shown in Fig. 10.

This kind of glass sculpture is yet in its infancy but no doubt it will mature into great things. It is capable of very superior finish— a finish not to be attained even upon the finest porcelain and is remarkable, not only for the sharpness of the outlines which are obtained but also for what artists term the fine texture of the figure work.

Anon., *Birmingham Daily Gazette*,
April 11, 1878

JOHN NORTHWOOD (1836–1902) dominated the early years of English cameo glass making. Born in Wordsley, he joined W. H., B. & J. Richardson about 1848, and here he learned the techniques of painting, enameling, and gilding. He left Richardson's in 1852 and worked for his elder brother until Benjamin Richardson took over the old works and re-engaged him. John Northwood was employed by Richardson until 1859, when he left to form a partnership with his brother Joseph, Henry Gething Richardson, and Thomas Guest. The new partnership was dissolved in 1860, when John and Joseph established a finishing shop known as J. & J. Northwood. Joseph was the manager, and John concentrated on developing new decorating techniques. In 1861, John introduced the Template Etching Machine, which produced decoration mechanically by tracing designs in the wax-coated glass through wooden templates. He also invented the Geometrical Etching Machine (1865), which operated without templates, and he capped these achievements by developing "white acid" (hydrofluoric acid and potassium carbonate or sodium carbonate). This dissolved the surface of glass without eating into it, thereby enabling him to decorate a cameo glass object from start to finish by etching alone. These inventions permitted the Northwoods to become the largest producers of etched glass in Stourbridge, employing between 50 and 60 finishers.

At the same time, John Northwood established his own reputation as an outstanding carver and engraver of glass. His *Elgin Vase*, commissioned in 1864 and completed in 1873, is a colorless glass amphora carved with a frieze of horses and riders based on the Elgin Marbles in the British Museum. Hailed as a masterpiece, the *Elgin Vase* was the forerunner of the English "Rock Crystal" style of deeply cut, engraved, and polished glass, which helped to establish Stourbridge as the center of the English fine glass industry.

In the 1860s and 1870s, J. & J. Northwood produced some of the best acid-etched glass in the Stourbridge region, and when cameo glass became popular, Northwood's became the finishing shop for Stevens & Williams.

Despite the efficiency of John Northwood's etching machines, the finest cameo glass was finished by hand. In 1873, Philip Pargeter (1826–1906), proprietor of the Red House Glass Works, told Northwood, "I believe I can make the Portland Vase if you can decorate it."[5] Pargeter's challenge echoed a sentiment expressed 26 years previously by Apsley Pellatt of the Falcon Glass Works, London. At a meeting of the Royal Institution on February 12, 1847, Pellatt exhibited a cased blank of the same shape and size as the original Portland Vase, "declaring that if any British engraver, of adequate skill, should propose to make an exact copy in glass ... his firm would undertake the manufacture of the vessel."[6]

Northwood accepted the challenge. The blank was blown at the Red House Glass Works by Daniel Hancox, assisted by Joseph Worrall, Charles Hancox (Daniel's son), and Benjamin Downing. It was entrusted to John Northwood, who spent three years carving it. The project almost foundered when, at an advanced stage, the vase cracked as a result of thermal shock when warm hands picked up the cold glass. Fortunately, the crack was repaired with an adhesive, and Northwood completed his task.

In his reminiscences, Thomas Woodall, who later became a member of the celebrated Woodall Team at Thomas Webb & Sons, recalled assisting Northwood in decorating the vase: "I made the first drawings and painted

17

FIG. 12. John Northwood's replica of the Portland Vase.

FIG. 13. John Northwood's drawing of the Portland Vase.

FIG. 14. *Perseus and Andromeda*, by John Northwood.

resist for acidizing this out which was a fairly long job as it was fairly thick in outer coating to get the necessary relief. Mr. John Northwood than [*sic*] took it in hand for carving with Steel points and the engravers lathe he used a little."[7] The drawing reproduced in Fig. 13 was formerly in the possession of the Northwood family, and it is firmly attributed to John Northwood. Presumably, Woodall was responsible for copying Northwood's design on the blank.

Another of Northwood's assistants was Edwin Grice. He worked on the handles of the Portland Vase, and in 1913 he recorded how the object was cracked:

> We had got the vase into a very forward condition, having worked upon it for two years, and we contemplated another journey to compare it with the original. Before we started early for London we had a terrible mishap. The night had been very frosty, and when the vase was being lifted carefully into the box something went crack. We afterwards found that the holding of the vase in warm hands had caused uneven expansion, producing a fracture. It put a damper on our spirits, as you may guess.[8]

Northwood's Portland Vase was not his first cameo glass vessel. About 1856, he produced a white-over-blue vase depicting Perseus and Andromeda. Unfortunately, the vase was broken and no longer exists, but the Rakow Library has a pencil sketch of the design, which was once in the collection of Kenneth Northwood, the artist's grandson. John Northwood also made an acid-etched, colorless version of the Portland Vase, perhaps in preparation for his attempt to produce a colored replica.

Northwood was instrumental in the completion of about 15 other replicas of the Portland Vase. This came about because he was the first person to apply to ceramics the techniques of engraving and polishing glass, and his etchers and engravers decorated large quantities of Wedgwood's popular Rockingham Ware. They also finished some of Wedgwood's copies of the Portland Vase made between 1877 and 1880. Northwood's role was to grind and polish Wedgwood's jasperware vases, and sometimes to improve the decoration by cutting. The relationship between Northwood and the Wedgwood company was difficult, as some of their correspondence (preserved in the Rakow Library) reveals. On occasion, Wedgwood sent defective vases in the expectation that Northwood could eliminate or conceal the defects, which sometimes proved to be impossible. Thus, on September 24, 1879, Wedgwood asked Northwood to "cut up the feet of cupid in the best way you can," and two days later, Northwood reported: "In cutting the Cupids [*sic*] foot, it was so hollow that the piece came off." If the correspondence at Corning is typical, the Wedgwood company was a demanding customer, and Northwood treated it with considerable patience.

To the best of our knowledge, John Northwood personally completed only nine pieces of cameo glass: the vase with Perseus and Andromeda (about 1856); the Portland Vase (1876); *The Milton Vase* (1878); three *tazza*s, with portraits of Sir Isaac Newton (1878), William Shakespeare (1880), and John Flaxman (1880); another *tazza* with a portrait of Shakespeare (see page 22); a pendant with a portrait of Shakespeare (after 1880); and the *Dennis* or *Pegasus Vase* (1882).

The Milton Vase, commissioned by Philip Pargeter in 1878, was inspired by John Milton's *Paradise Lost*. The vase depicts Adam and Eve in the Garden of Eden. Adam raises his arm and points to the figure on the other side of the vase, the archangel Michael.

FIG. 15. *The Milton Vase*, by John Northwood.

The three *tazza*s are decorated with portraits of famous practitioners of art, literature, and science. The representative of art was the sculptor John Flaxman (1755–1826), one of the protagonists of neo-classical taste in Britain. His portrait was taken from Wedgwood's jasperware medallion, which is said to have been modeled by Flaxman himself between 1787 and 1794. The *tazza* is signed "J.N. 1880." Literature is represented by William Shakespeare (1564–1616). This portrait, too, was taken from a Wedgwood medallion, modeled by William Hackwood. The representative of science was Sir Isaac Newton (1642–1727), who discovered the law of gravity. Again, the model was a jasperware medallion. The *tazza* is signed "J. Northwood 1878."

Northwood planned to carve a fourth *tazza*, in honor of engineering. This would have had a portrait of the Scottish engineer and inventor James Watt (1736–1819), but it was never completed. One of Northwood's drawings of the projected Watt *tazza* appears below.

The Newton and Flaxman *tazza*s were exhibited at the 1881 Art and Industrial Exhibition in Plymouth, England, where they won a silver medal. Later, all three *tazza*s, the replica of the Portland Vase, and *The Milton Vase* were exhibited together in Pargeter's London showroom.

A second Shakespeare *tazza*, then in the Rakow Collection, was shown in the 1982 exhibition of cameo glass at The Corning Museum of Glass, and it is illustrated in the catalog of that show. Undocumented and previously unpublished, the object was attributed to John Northwood—an attribution supported by Kenneth Northwood. (The present location of this object is unknown to me.)

FIG. 16. James Watt, drawn by John Northwood.

FIG. 17. Three *tazza*s carved by John Northwood: Newton, Shakespeare, and Flaxman.

FIG. 18. John Northwood's *Pegasus Vase.*

FIG. 19. Joseph Locke.

The *Pegasus Vase* was commissioned by Thomas Wilkes Webb of the Dennis Glass Works in Amblecote—hence its alternative name, the *Dennis Vase*. The object is an imitation of a large jasperware vase designed by Flaxman and made by Wedgwood in 1786. (Ten years later, Wedgwood presented it to the British Museum.) The vase shows Aurora, goddess of the dawn, in her chariot with attendants, and Amphitrite, goddess of the sea, in a shell drawn by sea horses. The cover has a large finial in the form of Pegasus, the winged horse of Greek and Roman mythology. The vase was exhibited, unfinished, at the Paris exposition of 1878, where it won a gold medal. Completed in 1882, it was sold by Webb to Tiffany & Co. of New York.

John Northwood was not the only skilled carver of cameo glasses in the Stourbridge area; one of his contemporaries was Joseph Locke (1846–1936), who began his working life as an apprentice at the Royal Worcester Porcelain Works. He entered the glass industry at the age of 19, when he won the competition to design a glass fireplace for Czar Alexander II. The czar had commissioned the fireplace from Guest Bros. of Brettel Lane. Later, Locke left Guest Bros. and joined Hodgetts, Richardson & Son, where he learned the technique of carving cameo glass from Alphonse Lechevrel. When the company decided to exhibit at the Paris exposition of 1878, Locke was persuaded to carve a replica of the Portland Vase. Although Locke worked on this task for a year, the replica was unfinished when the exposition opened. Nevertheless, it was greatly admired, and Locke was awarded a silver medal.

FIG. 20. Blank for a Portland Vase made by Hodgetts, Richardson & Son, 1878.

According to tradition, Hodgetts, Richardson & Son made 40 blanks for the Portland Vase project. Thirty-eight of these are said to have been defective, the 39th was usable, and the 40th survives in its unworked state.

Richardson's stand at the Paris exposition was breathtaking. It included not only Locke's Portland Vase and cameo glasses carved by Alphonse Lechevrel (see page 28), but also a great variety of cut, engraved, acid-etched, and threaded glass. (Joshua Hodgetts, another of Richardson's employees, had recently developed and patented the threading machine, which was used to apply long, spirally wound trails.)

Locke left Richardson's in 1879 and worked successively for Philip Pargeter's Red House Glass Works and another local firm, Webb & Corbett. In 1882, however, he emigrated to the United States, where he became an influential figure at the New England Glass Company of East Cambridge, Massachusetts. The proprietor of that company was Edward Drummond Libbey, who subsequently relocated it to Toledo, Ohio, in order to take advantage of the availability of natural gas there. Locke went with him, but in 1891 he moved to Pittsburgh, where he became head of design at the United States Glass Company and opened his own finishing shop. In America, Locke made cameo glasses and developed a number of highly successful varieties of Art Glass, including Amberina (patented in 1883), Pomona (1885), Wild Rose or Peachblow (1886), Agata (about 1887), and maize glassware (1889).

FIG. 21 (left). Joseph Locke's replica of the Portland Vase.

FIG. 22. *The Birth of Venus*, by Alphonse Lechevrel.

The Portland Vase continued to fascinate Stourbridge glassmakers, and about 1889 William Northwood (1857–1937), a nephew of John Northwood, carved a jar decorated with two Muses, basing his design on the form of the famous original.

Alphonse Lechevrel (1850–?) established a reputation in his native France as a medalist and gem engraver. In 1877, at the invitation of Benjamin Richardson, he went to Wordsley, where he worked for Hodgetts, Richardson & Son. Although he spent only two years in the Midlands, he exerted a powerful influence on local glass decorators. In 1878, Hodgetts, Richardson & Son exhibited four of his cameo glasses at the Exposition Universelle in Paris. All of these objects were vases, and each had a pair of vertical handles rising from the shoulder. Later, the handles were removed and George Woodall reworked the decoration. Two of the altered vases were exhibited at the Worcestershire Exhibition of 1882. The example shown in Fig. 22, which bears the signatures "AL 1877" (partly obliterated) and "Geo. Woodall," was reworked at an unknown date between 1878 and 1923. The title of the work, *The Birth of Venus*, is engraved on the base.

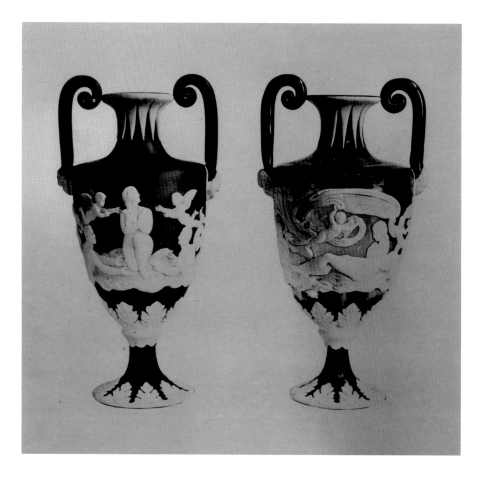

FIG. 23. Pair of vases carved by Alphonse Lechevrel.

FIG. 24. *Knight Fighting the Devil*, attributed to James Benjamin Hill.

The earliest English cameo glasses followed the color scheme of the original Portland Vase: opaque white over translucent deep blue. When English manufacturers began to produce cameo glass in other colors, they initially kept the white overlay but substituted other colors for the base glass.

In the plaque above, for example, the background is translucent greenish blue. The object is one of two unsigned and unfinished cameo plaques inherited by James T. Hill, Jr., and attributed to his grandfather, James Benjamin Hill (1850–1928), a designer, decorator, and etcher at Stevens & Williams. The acid-etched background has been neither ground nor polished, and the decoration is almost entirely lacking in fine detail.

In 1885, James O'Fallon noted how few cameo glass carvers were active. "Northwood, Grice, the brothers Woodall, and two or three others," he wrote, "are the only Englishmen yet employed in carving [cameo glass]." Evidently, making cameo glass was still a small business in 1885. O'Fallon explained the reason for this: "The artist who undertakes a work in glass that has to be in hand so long, is seldom or never able to devote all his time to it. As a matter of personal experience bearing on this, so far back as 1869 ... [I] commenced a vase, since occasionally left aside for sake of pressing calls on [my] time, yet, to satisfactorily finish carving it, about two years more of consecutive labour, reckoned seven hours daily, would be necessary."[9]

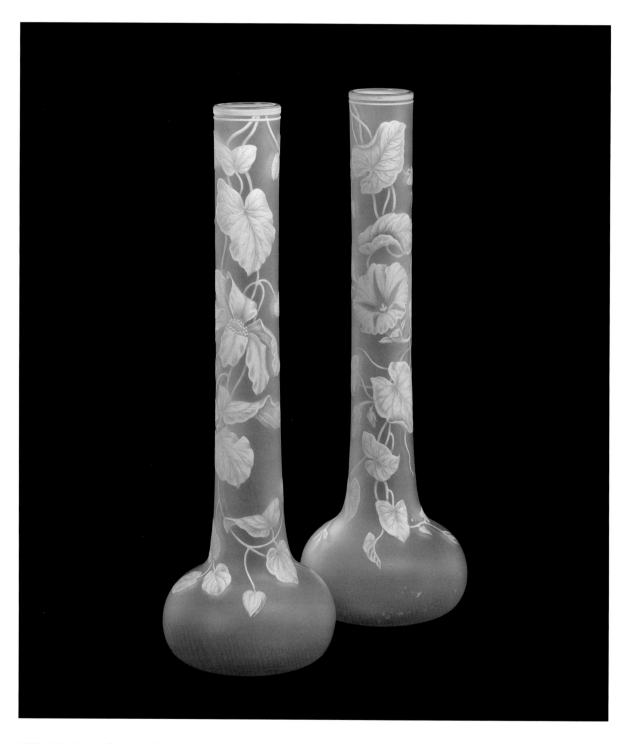

FIG. 25. Pair of vases, about 1880.

IN SPITE OF Richardson's outstanding display at the 1878 Paris exhibition, that firm was soon eclipsed by two other Stourbridge companies, Stevens & Williams and Thomas Webb & Sons. John Northwood was appointed artistic director of the Stevens & Williams company in 1881, and shortly after this the company began to produce cameo glass in a wide range of shapes and colors. It continued to make large numbers of cameo glasses throughout the 1880s, but it reduced production in the 1890s. Some of the company's blanks were decorated on the premises, while others were farmed out to J. & J. Northwood, whose finishing shop in Wordsley employed a number of talented craftsmen, including William Northwood and Joshua Hodgetts.

Of all the craftsmen employed by Stevens & Williams, none was more remarkable than Frederick Carder (1863–1963). Carder was born in Kingswinford. While still a boy, he joined his grandfather's Leys Pottery in Brierley Hill, and at the same time, he attended night school to study

art and chemistry, metallurgy, and chemical engineering. His grandfather died in 1878, and Carder, unhappy with the new management, resolved to leave the Leys Pottery. The following year, he visited John Northwood's studio and saw the replica of the Portland Vase. "Struck with the possibilities of glass," Carder made up his mind to "get into the business."[10] In 1880, he joined Stevens & Williams as a designer. At that time, the company bought the colored glass it needed for casing its own colorless glass. Lacking a machine shop, it also purchased molds for casting. Carder was permitted to acquire a small furnace to experiment with melting colored glass, and a lathe to make models for molds. "What with making models, designing, and conducting experiments in making colored glasses, I was kept quite busy," he recalled.[11] In 1881, Carder's mentor, John Northwood, was appointed director of design at Stevens & Williams, and this cemented Carder's relationship with the Stourbridge factory, where he remained for more than 20 years.

FIG. 26. Frederick Carder.

In 1902, the South Staffordshire County Council commissioned Carder to visit and report on glass factories in Germany and Austria—an action designed to improve the competitiveness of the Stourbridge manufacturers. The following year, the same organization sent him to the United States. Carder visited Pittsburgh, Washington, and Corning, where he toured the Corning Glass Works (which he promptly dubbed the "Smokestack University") and met with T. G. Hawkes of the glass cutting firm T. G. Hawkes & Co. This was not the first occasion on which Carder and Hawkes had done business; for some time, Stevens & Williams had been selling Hawkes blanks for his cutting shop. Now, however, Carder and Hawkes joined forces and founded Steuben Glass Works (Corning is in Steuben County), with Hawkes as the majority shareholder and Carder as his junior partner and manager. The new factory was amazingly prolific. Carder experimented with batches and designed new shapes. Between 1903 and 1932 (when Carder left the company), Steuben produced more than 7,000 designs—at an average rate of almost one every working day!

FIG. 27. Two vases carved by Frederick Carder, about 1890.

FIG. 28. *The Great Tazza*, carved by the Woodall Team, about 1889.

THOMAS WEBB (1802–1869) entered the glass industry in 1829, when he joined Benjamin Richardson and William Haden Richardson in founding Webb & Richardsons. The partnership lasted seven years. In 1835, Webb inherited his father's share in another glassworks, Shepherd and Webb. The following year, he bought out his partner, and in 1837 the Richardsons acquired Webb's share in Webb & Richardsons. After the completion of the transaction, Webb founded Thomas Webb & Sons. The new company quickly rose to prominence. A contributor to *The Art Union* of April 1846 described his visit to Webb's factory and commented that "in clearness and purity [of lead glass], he is confessedly unsurpassed in Europe." Webb consolidated his reputation in 1851, when his cut glass won a medal at the Great Exhibition in London. In 1856, he acquired the Dennis estate in Amblecote and he built the Dennis Glass Works. Following his retirement in 1866, the company was run by

three of his sons, Thomas Wilkes Webb, Charles Webb, and Walter Wilkes Webb.

Thomas Wilkes Webb (1837–1891) was the driving force. At the Paris exhibition of 1878, his chandeliers won a prize for the company and appointment to the Legion of Honor for Webb himself. According to the catalog of the exhibition, "Messrs. Thomas Webb & Co., of Stourbridge, are the best makers of Crystal Glass in England, and consequently, in the world; for if Germany and France surpass us in the production of coloured glass, they are far behind us in the pure metal, worked or unworked." The company also won first prizes and gold medals at the Sydney and Melbourne, Australia, exhibitions of 1880 and 1881. In the 27 years when Thomas Wilkes Webb was in charge, the Dennis Glass Works produced more than 10,000 designs, and from 1874 to 1890 alone, it developed 54 new colored glasses. Some of these products were extremely difficult or laborious to make; "Old

FIG. 29. The Woodall Team working on *The Great Tazza*.

Ivory," for example, was gilded, painted, enameled, stained, engraved, carved, perforated, embedded with jewels, cased, and etched!

Like Benjamin Richardson, Thomas Wilkes Webb employed some of the most talented decorators of the day. Some of these craftsmen came from Ireland, France, and Bohemia. They included Frederick Engelbert Kny and his son Ludwig, the master "Rock Crystal" engraver William Fritsche (1853–1924), Jules Barbe, and F. Kretschman. The greatest of Webb's decorators, however, were George Woodall (1850–1925), his brother Thomas, and the other members of the Woodall Team: Harry Davis, Jacob Facer, James O'Fallon, Thomas Farmer, John Thomas Fereday, William Hill, and Francis Smith.

The publicity surrounding the production in Wordsley of *two* Portland Vase replicas (Northwood's and Locke's) and other cameo glasses did not go unnoticed in Amblecote, and Thomas Wilkes Webb experimented at length with acids, cutting, and engraving. Eventually, Webb was satisfied, and about 1880 his company began to produce cameo glass.

Cameo glass became extremely fashionable, and the demand taxed even the resources of Thomas Webb & Sons. Every available engraver was hired to work overtime and on Saturdays, and the Woodall Team expanded until it included about 70 engravers! Others producing cameo glass at this time included Frederick Stuart of Stuart & Sons, who acquired Philip Pargeter's Red House Glass Works in 1881 and introduced "Medallion Cameo" glass (with pads of colored glass on a colorless body) in 1887, and Boulton & Mills.

The Webb firm's output was prodigious. It included not only "classical" designs, such as those of the Woodalls, but also imitations of Chinese cameo glass and Japanese snuff bottles. The Corning collection contains an outstanding example of an object with "Oriental" decoration: a gilded and enameled gourd-shaped vase that was decorated by Kretschman and Barbe about 1890.

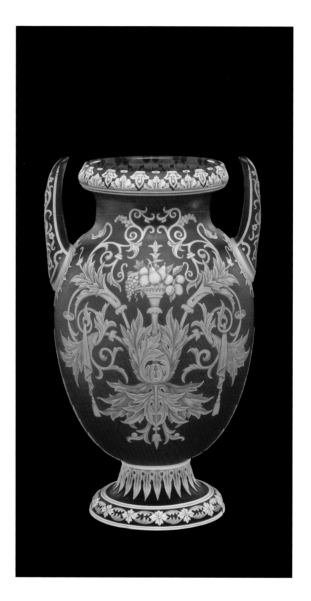

FIG. 30. Vase, probably carved by the Woodall Team, about 1880–1890.

FIG. 32. *Nymph in a Crescent Moon* or *Luna*, attributed to Ludwig Kny.

Jules Barbe was a French gilder and enameler. He exhibited his work at the Paris exposition of 1878, and a year later he went to Stourbridge. Barbe was employed at the Dennis Glass Works, where he introduced the "raised" gilded decoration shown opposite. This consisted of a paste made of gold, mercury, and other ingredients. It was painted on the glass and fired in a muffle furnace fueled with oak wood. After annealing, the gilding was burnished with spun glass brushes. Barbe worked for Webb's until 1901, when he became a free-lance decorator. F. Kretsch-

FIG. 31. Gourd vase, 1888.

man, who engraved the gourd vase, is known to have lived in the Stourbridge area from 1886 to 1892.

Frederick Engelbert Kny was one of several Bohemian glassworkers employed at the Dennis Glass Works (William Fritsche was another). Kny came to Amblecote in 1860, and, like Fritsche, he became a skilled engraver of colorless glasses decorated in the high-relief "Rock Crystal" style. Among the best known of his works was the *Elgin Jug* (1873), a claret jug decorated with friezes of horsemen copied from Flaxman's illustrations for Homer's *Iliad* and *Odyssey*. The *Elgin Jug*—not to be confused with John Northwood's *Elgin Vase* (see page 17)—was exhibited at the Paris exhibition of 1878.

George and Thomas Woodall left school at the age of about 12 and became apprentices at J. & J. Northwood. At the same time they attended evening classes at the local art school, where Thomas later became an instructor. After completing their apprenticeships, first Thomas and later George moved to the Dennis Glass Works, where they were employed primarily as designers.

The Woodalls made two important innovations. One was their extensive use of the cutting wheel, which greatly speeded up the process of decorating cameo glass; the other was their overlay of white glass with a bluish tint, which, when thinned over burgundy or brown base glass, allowed them to achieve a much greater range of shading than was possible with other white glasses.

FIG. 33. *The Origin of Painting*, carved by George Woodall, 1884.

FIG. 34. *Venus and Cupid*, by George Woodall.

George Woodall was an eclectic designer, and he derived his designs from a variety of printed sources. He made frequent use, for example, of Countess Albrizzi's publication *The Works of Antonio Canova* (1824), which illustrated the neo-classical works of this influential Italian sculptor (1757–1822). Woodall's other sources included *Vases from the Collection of Sir Henry Englefield, Bart., Drawn and Engraved by H. Moses, Etchings and Engravings of Grecian and Roman Architectural Ornament* by C. H. Tatham (1863), and Owen Jones's *Examples of Chinese Ornament* (1867), which inspired the design of *The Great Tazza* (Fig. 28) and *The Great Dish* (frontispiece).

On January 20, 1912, a local newspaper, the *County Express*, published an interview with George Woodall. This article is a mine of information about Woodall himself and the production of cameo glass at Thomas Webb & Sons. It describes one of Woodall's innovations, which appears to advantage on the *Aphrodite* plaque. "The late Mr. John Northwood," the article states, "had in his work used opaque white colour, which remained solely white, to however deep an extent it was carved. Mr. George Woodall adopted as his medium a different metal, a white with a blue tinge, which when carved down upon the brown background became semi-transparent and of a most delicate and beautiful blue, thus increasing enormously the range of the artist's possibility of scene-painting."

FIG. 35. George Woodall's *Aphrodite*, 1892.

FIG. 36. George Woodall's medallions of Dr. and Mrs. Samuel Parkes Cadman.

George Woodall's exceptional skill as a cameo glass artist is reflected in his miniature portraits. He carved eight portraits: Lord Kelvin (in the collection of the Royal Society of London), Mrs. Martin (location unknown), Judge and Mrs. Winans (location unknown; it was formerly in the collection of Thomas Webb & Sons), the "Armenian Girl" (at Broadfield House Glass Museum, Dudley, England), Prime Minister Gladstone (in the collection of Mr. and Mrs. Billy Hitt), and Dr. and Mrs. Samuel Parkes Cadman. The Cadman plaques are among the most sensitively carved examples of English cameo glass. They depict a highly successful evangelist and his wife. Dr. Cadman (1864–1936) was related to George Woodall through his mother, who was Woodall's sister-in-law. A cleric, he migrated to the United States in 1890 and served congregations in Yonkers, Millbrook, and Brooklyn, New York. He began his radio ministry in 1923, and this continued until his death in 1936. Cadman Plaza and Cadman Memorial Church in Brooklyn are named for him.

FIG. 37. Potpourri jar, about 1880–1890.

A WOODALL MISCELLANY

The following pages show a selection of cameo glass decorated by George Woodall and the Woodall Team between about 1880 and 1910.

FIG. 38. George Woodall in his studio, about 1885.

The *Muses* is decorated with five standing figures—more than on any other Woodall composition, apart from the *Moorish Bathers*. The figures are five of the nine Muses: Euterpe (the Muse of music or flute playing), Erato (lyric and love poetry), Terpsichore (dance and choral song), Clio (history), and Thalia (comedy). The designer (perhaps Woodall) made a complete hash of the iconography. Euterpe (identified by an inscription) is shown with a stringed instrument instead of flutes, Thalia has flutes instead of a comic mask, and Clio holds a lyre instead of a scroll.

FIG. 39. *The Muses*, 1885.

In Fig. 41, Cleopatra is shown standing in front of an elaborately carved Egyptian temple. She holds a *sistrum* (a musical instrument used in religious rituals) in her right hand. The vase is marked on the base: "THOMAS WEBB & SONS / GEM / CAMEO / W2848 CLEOPATRA."

FIG. 40 (left). *Venus and Cupid*, carved by George Woodall, 1884.

FIG. 41. *Cleopatra*, carved by George Woodall, 1896.

This is a fine example of the work of Thomas and George Woodall when they worked as partners. Thomas Woodall (1849–1926), George's elder brother, was also a skilled cameo carver. When the two brothers collaborated on a piece, George carved or completed carving the figures and Thomas designed and carved the borders. The Woodalls signed pieces jointly from about 1880 to 1895, when, for unknown reasons, they quarreled. This is a well-documented example of their collaboration, since the base is signed "T. & G. WOODALL. DES. & SCULPS." The base also bears the impressed mark "THOMAS WEBB & SONS / GEM / CAMEO."

FIG. 42. *A Maid of Athens*, by Thomas and George Woodall.

Inspiration, signed "G. Woodall," has the following acid-etched marks under the base: "THOMAS WEBB & SONS / GEM / CAMEO" and "THEODORE B. STARR / NEW / YORK." The second mark indicates that the vase was made for the American market.

FIG. 43. George Woodall's *Inspiration*.

FIG. 44. George Woodall in his studio, after 1898.

FIG. 45. *Moorish Bathers*, by George Woodall, 1898.

Moorish Bathers is George Woodall's master-piece. It was begun about 1890 and completed in 1898. Acquired by the Hon. George Brook-man of Adelaide, Australia, it narrowly escaped destruction when the Brookmans' house was destroyed by fire.

FIG. 46. *Flora*, by Thomas and George Woodall.

The *Flora* plaque is signed "T. & G. Woodall" at the lower right. The back has the acid-etched mark "THOMAS WEBB & SONS" in an arc above "GEM / CAMEO," and "WEBB" in a four-lobed mark below.

FIG. 47. George Woodall's *Andromache*, 1902.

Andromache was the wife of Hector, son of King Priam of Troy. In Homer's *Iliad*, all of Andromache's relatives died during or immediately after the capture of Troy by the Greeks. Andromache herself was taken prisoner and given to Neoptolemus, the son of Achilles, who took her back to his home in Epirus. The plaque is inscribed "ANDROMACHE" at the bottom of the frame, and it is signed "Geo. Woodall" on the pavement. The panel, completed in October 1902, was sold in February 1917.

This lamp base, or one very similar to it, appears, together with *The Great Tazza*, in a photograph of glass in Thomas Goode & Co.'s London showroom about 1891. It is decorated with an overall Chinese floral and geometric pattern that includes the symbol for "long life and happiness."

FIG. 48. Lamp base, probably carved by the Woodall Team.

FIG. 49. The London showroom of Thomas Goode & Co.

The so-called *Dancing Girl* (the original name is unknown) is also signed "G. Woodall," and it has the acid-etched mark "THOMAS WEBB & SONS / GEM / CAMEO." The vase appears to have a reddish purple layer sandwiched between the opaque white and blue glasses. This, however, is an illusion, apparently created by the opalescent quality of the white overlay.

FIG. 50. *The Dancing Girl*, carved by George Woodall.

George Woodall remained at Thomas Webb & Sons until his retirement in 1911, and the *Antarctic* vase is one of the last pieces he produced for the company. After he retired, Woodall continued to carve cameo glasses in his studio in Kingswinford until his death in 1925.

FIG. 51. *Antarctic*, designed and carved by George Woodall.

FIG. 52. *Aphrodite and Attendants*, by John Northwood II.

BY THE END of the 19th century, most cameo glass was made by machines that used the acid etching process to mass-produce decorative objects. Fewer and fewer pieces were carved by hand. Indeed, the latest hand-finished display pieces were decorated by craftsmen whose products were no longer commercially viable. John Northwood II's plaque depicting Aphrodite and her attendants is a case in point.

John Northwood II (1870–1960) became an assistant to his father at Stevens & Williams in 1881–1882 and eventually succeeded him as the company's art director and plant manager. His plaque shows the goddess Aphrodite, who, according to Greek mythology, was born by rising naked from the sea, then rode to land on a scallop shell. She is surrounded by attendants. Eros flies behind her. The figures in front of her are cupids, those on the viewer's left are a sea nymph and a hippocamp (a mythical creature with the head and forequarters of a horse and the tail of a dolphin), and those on the viewer's right are another sea nymph and a triton. Behind the goddess's shell is a second triton blowing on a conch shell. (Tritons are demigods with the head and torso of a man and the tail of a fish.)

The design was chosen by John Northwood I, whose replica of the ancient Roman Portland Vase, completed in 1876, had an enormous influence on the popularity of cameo glass in Victorian Britain. John Northwood II began to carve the Aphrodite plaque when he was 17 years old, stopped after 18 months of work, and did not resume the task until after his father's death in 1902. The plaque was completed four years later, but shortly after this it fell from a table and broke.

The Aphrodite plaque is one of the last major cameo glasses made in the Stourbridge region. In his 1912 interview in the *County Express* (see page 40), George Woodall described the demise of the English cameo glass industry:

> At one time ... there were about 70 people assisting my brother and myself in doing this work. The glass engraving trade was then at a very low ebb, and we could get as many engravers as we wanted. Other firms in the [Stourbridge] district also embarked upon the trade, until there were as many as 150 people in the district engaged in it. There continued to be a good market for the ornaments till at length our trade was ruined by the foreigner. A German imitation came into vogue, a sort of enamel painting so like the glass that those unacquainted with the industry could not tell the difference. The imitation goods were sold at one tenth of the price of the genuine, and our trade died away, after lasting some twenty years [from 1880 to 1900]."

FURTHER READING

Beard, Geoffrey W. *Nineteenth Century Cameo Glass.* Newport, Monmouthshire: The Ceramic Book Co., 1956.

Braby, Michael. "Rivalling the Romans." *Art & Antiques,* September 6, 1975, pp. 26–29.

Duffy, E. Mary. "Philip Pargeter and John Northwood I, Cameo Glass Pioneers." *Antiques,* v. 82, no. 6, December 1962, pp. 639–641.

English Nineteenth Century Cameo Glass from the Collection of Mr. and Mrs. Albert Christian Revi (exhibition catalog). Corning: The Corning Museum of Glass, 1963.

Eveson, S. R. "Reflections: Sixty Years with the Crystal Glass Industry. Part 2." *Glass Technology,* v. 31, no. 2, April 1990, pp. 49–55.

Farrar, Estelle Sinclaire. "John Northwood and English Cameo Glass." *Arts & Antiques,* v. 4, no. 4, July/August 1981, pp. 50–55.

Gaines, Edith. "Collector's Notes: Cameo-Glass Portraits—A First." *Arts,* v. 109, no. 6, June 1976, p. 1171.

Gardner, Paul V. *The Glass of Frederick Carder.* New York: Crown Publishers, Inc., 1971.

__. *Frederick Carder: Portrait of a Glassmaker* (exhibition catalog). Corning: The Corning Museum of Glass and The Rockwell Museum, 1985.

Goldstein, Sidney M., Leonard S. Rakow, and Juliette K. Rakow. *Cameo Glass: Masterpieces from 2000 Years of Glassmaking* (exhibition catalog). Corning: The Corning Museum of Glass, 1982.

Grover, Ray and Lee. *Carved and Decorated European Art Glass.* Rutland, Vermont: Charles E. Tuttle Company, 1970.

__. *English Cameo Glass.* New York: Crown Publishers, 1980.

Haden, H. Jack. *Artists in Cameo Glass, Incorporating Thomas Woodall's Memoirs.* Kingswinford: The Black Country Society, 1993.

Hajdamach, Charles R. *British Glass, 1800–1914.* Woodbridge: Antique Collectors' Club, 1991.

Lanmon, Dwight P. "John Northwood and Wedgwood: Some Correspondence." *Ars Ceramica,* v. 2, 1985, pp. 18–20.

Northwood, John II. "Noteworthy Productions of the Glass Craftsman's Art. I. The Reproduction of the Portland Vase." *Journal of the Society of Glass Technology,* v. 8, 1924, pp. 85–92.

__. "Stourbridge Cameo Glass." *Notes and News of the Society of Glass Technology,* v. 33, 1949, pp. 106–113.

__. *John Northwood—His Contribution to the Stourbridge Flint Glass Industry, 1850–1902.* Stourbridge: Mark + Moody, 1958.

O'Fallon, J. M. "Glass Carving as an Art." *Art Journal,* December 1885, pp. 378–380.

Rakow, Leonard S. and Juliette K. "The Glass Replicas of the Portland Vase." *Journal of Glass Studies,* v. 24, 1982, pp. 49–56.

Revi, Albert Christian. *Nineteenth Century Glass—Its Genesis and Development.* New York, Edinburgh, and Toronto: Thomas Nelson and Sons, 1959.

Silverman, Alexander. "Joseph Locke, Artist." *The Glass Industry,* v. 17, no. 8, August 1936, pp. 272–275.

Turner, W. E. S. "Noteworthy Productions of the Glass Craftsman's Art, II. Mr. John Northwood's Plaque of *Aphrodite.*" *Journal of the Society of Glass Technology,* v. 8, 1924, pp. 92T–93T.

Wakefield, Hugh. *Nineteenth Century British Glass.* London: Faber and Faber, 1961.

Woodward, H. W. *Art, Fear and Mystery: The Story of Thomas Webb & Sons Glassmakers.* Stourbridge: Mark + Moody, 1978.

NOTES ON THE ILLUSTRATIONS

All objects are in The Corning Museum of Glass unless otherwise indicated.

Frontispiece. *The Great Dish*. Amblecote, Thomas Webb & Sons, carved by the Woodall Team, about 1889. D. 38 cm (15 in). 92.2.9. Formerly in the collection of Dr. and Mrs. Leonard S. Rakow. Bequest of Mrs. Rakow.

1. The Portland Vase. Roman Empire, probably Italy, late 1st century B.C. H. 24.8 cm (9 13/16 in). British Museum, Department of Greek and Roman Antiquities, 1945.9-27.1. Reproduced by courtesy of the British Museum.

2. Replica of the Portland Vase. Etruria, Josiah Wedgwood, about 1790. Jasperware. H. 25.8 cm (10 3/16 in). 92.7.2. Formerly in the collections of Richard Barker, members of the Barker family, and Dr. and Mrs. Leonard S. Rakow. Clara S. Peck Endowment Purchase.

This example (number 3) of Wedgwood's "first edition" of replicas of the Portland Vase was made for Richard Barker, a friend of Thomas Bentley, one of the potter's partners.

3. The Stourbridge area.

4. Vase (unfinished). Stourbridge, Joshua Hodgetts, 1932. H. 46.5 cm (18 3/8 in). 69.2.2.

5. *Cleopatra*. George Woodall, about 1880. Pencil on brown paper. H. 42.2 cm (16 5/8 in). Formerly in the collections of Alice Woodall and Dr. and Mrs. Leonard S. Rakow. Gift of Mrs. Rakow in memory of Dr. Rakow.

6. *Antony and Cleopatra*. Amblecote, Thomas Webb & Sons, about 1895. D. 47.7 cm (18 13/16 in). 89.2.6. Formerly in the collection of Dr. and Mrs. Leonard S. Rakow. Gift of Mrs. Rakow in memory of Dr. Rakow.

7. *The Attack* (unfinished). Amblecote, Thomas Webb & Sons, carved by Thomas and George Woodall, about 1899. Photograph. Formerly in the collection of Dr. and Mrs. Leonard S. Rakow. Bequest of Mrs. Rakow.

A different version of *The Attack* is in the collection of Mr. and Mrs. Billy Hitt. It is possible that the plaque illustrated here, which is known only from photographs, is the object mentioned in *The Lady*, June 15, 1899: "When the artist had reached the last stage but one in the original specimen, a flaw was discovered in the glass, and the whole of the work, which had occupied him for many months, had to be recommenced on a fresh piece of glass."

8. *The Attack* at an early stage of carving. Amblecote, Thomas Webb & Sons, carved by Thomas and George Woodall, about 1899. Photograph. Formerly in the collection of Dr. and Mrs. Leonard S. Rakow. Bequest of Mrs. Rakow.

9. *The Immortality of the Arts*. Brierley Hill, Stevens & Williams, carved by Frederick Carder (signed), 1887. D. 33 cm (13 in). 69.2.39. Formerly in the collections of Frederick Carder and his daughter, Mrs. Gladys Welles. Bequest of Mrs. Welles.

The design is taken from a relief by the French sculptor Antonin Mercié (1845–1916).

10. Graver. Stourbridge, early 20th century. Brass tool with steel point in adjustable jaws, formerly owned by Frederick Carder. L. 13 cm (5 1/4 in). 55.7.1.

11. Frederick Carder's hands, demonstrating how he carved *The Immortality of the Arts* using the graver shown in Fig. 10.

12. Replica of the Portland Vase. Wordsley, carved by John Northwood from a blank made at the Red House Glass Works of Philip Pargeter, 1873–1876. H. 25 cm (9 13/16 in). 92.2.7. Formerly in the collections of Philip Pargeter, other members of the Pargeter family, and Dr. and Mrs. Leonard S. Rakow. Bequest of Mrs. Rakow.

13. The Portland Vase. John Northwood, about 1873. Pencil on paper. H. 16.5 cm (6 1/2 in). Formerly in the collections of Kenneth Northwood and Dr. and Mrs. Leonard S. Rakow. Bequest of Mrs. Rakow.

14. *Perseus and Andromeda.* John Northwood, about 1860. H. 28.2 cm (11 1/8 in). Formerly in the collections of Kenneth Northwood and Dr. and Mrs. Leonard S. Rakow. Bequest of Mrs. Rakow.

15. *The Milton Vase.* Wordsley, carved by John Northwood, 1876. H. 33 cm (13 in). Collection of Mr. and Mrs. Billy Hitt. Reproduced by courtesy of Mr. and Mrs. Hitt.

16. *James Watt.* John Northwood, about 1880. Pencil on paper. H. 12.5 cm (4 15/16 in).

17. Three *tazza*s: Newton, Shakespeare, and Flaxman. Wordsley, carved by John Northwood, 1878–1880. D. (each) 23.5 cm (9 1/4 in). 92.2.11–13. Formerly in the collections of Philip Pargeter, other members of the Pargeter family, and Dr. and Mrs. Leonard S. Rakow. Bequest of Mrs. Rakow.

18. *Pegasus Vase.* Wordsley, carved by John Northwood, 1882 (signed and dated). H. 53.5 cm (21 1/16 in). The National Gallery of American Art, Smithsonian Institution. Gift of John Gellatly. Reproduced by courtesy of the National Gallery of American Art.

19. Joseph Locke. This card, bearing a photograph and signature, is Locke's pass to the Paris exhibition of 1878. Reproduced by courtesy of Joseph H. Locke.

20. Blank for a Portland Vase. Wordsley, Hodgetts, Richardson & Son, 1878. H. 25.3 cm (9 15/16 in). 92.2.16. Clara S. Peck Endowment Purchase.

21. Replica of the Portland Vase. Wordsley, Hodgetts, Richardson & Son, carved by Joseph Locke, 1878 (signed and dated). H. 25.3 cm (9 15/16 in). 92.2.15. Formerly in the collections of Mr. and Mrs. Albert C. Revi and Dr. and Mrs. Leonard S. Rakow. Clara S. Peck Endowment Purchase.

22. *The Birth of Venus.* Wordsley, Hodgetts, Richardson & Son, carved by Alphonse Lechevrel (signed), 1877; handles removed and additional cutting by George Woodall (also signed), possibly as late as 1923. H. 28.5 cm (11 1/4 in). 93.2.6. Formerly in the collections of Mr. and Mrs. Albert C. Revi and Dr. and Mrs. Leonard S. Rakow.

23. Pair of vases. Wordsley, Hodgetts, Richardson & Son, carved by Alphonse Lechevrel. H. 14.8 cm (5 7/8 in). Formerly in the collection of Dr. and Mrs. Leonard S. Rakow. Bequest of Mrs. Rakow.

The Birth of Venus appears on the right in this photograph, which was taken about the time of the 1878 Paris exhibition.

24. *Knight Fighting the Devil.* Probably Wordsley, carving attributed to James Benjamin Hill, about 1880. D. 29.9 cm (11 13/16 in). 92.2.1. Formerly in the collections of James T. Hill, Jr. (grandson of James Benjamin Hill), and Dr. and Mrs. Leonard S. Rakow. Gift of Mrs. Rakow in memory of Dr. Rakow.

25. Pair of vases. Stourbridge, Stevens & Williams, about 1880. H. 38.2 cm, 38 cm (15 in, 14 15/16 in). 89.2.23A, B. Formerly in the collection of Dr. and Mrs. Leonard S. Rakow. Gift of Mrs. Rakow in memory of Dr. Rakow.

26. Frederick Carder, about 1921. Reproduced by courtesy of Department of Archives and Records Management, Corning Incorporated.

27. Two vases. Stourbridge, Stevens & Williams, carved by Frederick Carder, about 1890. H. 15.8 cm, 14.3 cm (6 13/16 in, 5 5/8 in). 69.2.45, 55.2.6. Bequest of Mrs. Gillett Welles (larger vase) and gift of Frederick Carder.

28. *The Great Tazza*. Amblecote, Thomas Webb & Sons, carved by the Woodall Team, about 1889. H. 38.9 cm (15 5/16 in). 92.2.8. Formerly in the collection of Dr. and Mrs. Leonard S. Rakow. Bequest of Mrs. Rakow.

29. The Woodall Team working on *The Great Tazza*. Photograph, about 1889. H. 14.9 cm (5 7/8 in). Formerly in the collection of Dr. and Mrs. Leonard S. Rakow. Bequest of Mrs. Rakow.

This photograph, from an album that belonged to Alice Woodall, shows (clockwise from left) William Hill, Thomas Farmer, Harry Davis, John Thomas Fereday, Thomas Woodall, and George Woodall.

30. Vase. Amblecote, Thomas Webb & Sons, probably carved by the Woodall Team, about 1880–1890. H. 29.2 cm (11 1/2 in). 89.2.11. Formerly in the collection of Dr. and Mrs. Leonard S. Rakow. Gift of Mrs. Rakow in memory of Dr. Rakow.

31. Gourd vase. Amblecote, Thomas Webb & Sons, carved by F. Kretschman, enameled and gilded by Jules Barbe, 1888. H. 22.9 cm (8 7/8 in). 89.2.7. Formerly in the collections of Arthur Sussel and Dr. and Mrs. Leonard S. Rakow. Gift of Mrs. Rakow in memory of Dr. Rakow.

32. *Nymph in a Crescent Moon* or *Luna*. Probably Amblecote, carving attributed to Ludwig Kny, about 1888. D. 24.4 cm (9 5/8 in). 89.2.17. Formerly in the collections of Mrs. Ludwig Kny and Dr. and Mrs. Leonard S. Rakow. Gift of Mrs. Rakow in memory of Dr. Rakow.

33. *The Origin of Painting*. Amblecote, Thomas Webb & Sons, carved by George Woodall, 1884 (signed and dated). D. 25.5 cm (10 in). 89.2.15. Formerly in the collection of Dr. and Mrs. Leonard S. Rakow. Gift of Mrs. Rakow in memory of Dr. Rakow.

The composition was inspired by *The Maid of Corinth*, a painting by the English artist Joseph Wright (1734–1797), usually known as "Wright of Derby." The plaque is signed "G. WOODALL / 1884."

34. *Venus and Cupid*. Stourbridge, carved by George Woodall (signed), probably 1908. D. 46 cm (18 1/8 in). 65.2.19.

35. *Aphrodite*. Amblecote, Thomas Webb & Sons, carved by George Woodall, 1892 (signed and dated). D. 33.3 cm (13 1/8 in). 89.2.16. Formerly in the Nettlefold Collection and the collections of Mr. and Mrs. Albert C. Revi and Dr. and Mrs. Leonard S. Rakow. Gift of Mrs. Rakow in memory of Dr. Rakow.

The plaque is inscribed at the lower right "G. Woodall. 1892." The reverse has three acid-etched inscriptions: "APHRODITE," "THOMAS WEBB & SONS / GEM / CAMEO," and "WEBB." It was exhibited at the World's Columbian Exposition in Chicago in 1893.

36. Two medallions: Dr. and Mrs. Samuel Parkes Cadman. Amblecote, Thomas Webb & Sons, carved by George Woodall, about 1895. H. (each) 15.7 cm (6 3/16 in). 92.2.2A, B. Formerly in the collection of Dr. and Mrs. Leonard S. Rakow. Gift of Mrs. Rakow in memory of Dr. Rakow.

37. Potpourri jar. Amblecote, Thomas Webb & Sons, carved by George or Thomas Woodall, 1880–1890. H. 8.6 cm (3 3/8 in). 92.2.3. Formerly in the collection of Dr. and Mrs. Leonard S. Rakow. Gift of Seymour Salem.

38. George Woodall in his studio. Photograph, about 1885. Formerly in the collection of Dr. and Mrs. Leonard S. Rakow. Bequest of Mrs. Rakow.

39. *The Muses.* Amblecote, Thomas Webb & Sons, carved by Thomas and George Woodall, about 1885. H. 19.8 cm (7 13/16 in). 89.2.12. Formerly in the collection of Dr. and Mrs. Leonard S. Rakow. Gift of Mrs. Rakow in memory of Dr. Rakow.

40. *Venus and Cupid.* Amblecote, Thomas Webb & Sons, carved by George Woodall, 1884 (signed and dated). D. 33.1 cm (13 in). 89.2.8. Formerly in the collection of Dr. and Mrs. Leonard S. Rakow. Gift of Mrs. Rakow in memory of Dr. Rakow.

41. *Cleopatra.* Amblecote, Thomas Webb & Sons, carved by George Woodall (signed), 1896. H. 27.5 cm (10 13/16 in). 81.2.27. Formerly in the collections of E. L. Paget and Dr. and Mrs. Leonard S. Rakow. Gift of Dr. and Mrs. Rakow.

42. *A Maid of Athens.* Amblecote, Thomas Webb & Sons, carved by Thomas and George Woodall (signed), about 1885. H. 26.1 cm (10 1/4 in). 89.2.14. Formerly in the collections of Mr. and Mrs. Albert C. Revi and Dr. and Mrs. Leonard S. Rakow. Gift of Mrs. Rakow in memory of Dr. Rakow.

43. *Inspiration.* Amblecote, Thomas Webb & Sons, carved by George Woodall (signed), about 1880–1890. H. 30.2 cm (11 7/8 in). 80.2.5. Gift of Dr. and Mrs. Leonard S. Rakow.

44. George Woodall in his studio. Photograph, 1898 or later. Formerly in the collection of Dr. and Mrs. Leonard S. Rakow. Bequest of Mrs. Rakow.

45. *Moorish Bathers.* Amblecote, Thomas Webb & Sons, carved and engraved by George Woodall (signed), 1898. D. 46.3 cm (18 1/4 in). 92.2.10. Formerly in the collections of Mr. and Mrs. Albert C. Revi and Dr. and Mrs. Leonard S. Rakow. Bequest of Mrs. Rakow.

46. *Flora.* Amblecote, Thomas Webb & Sons, carved and engraved by Thomas and George Woodall (signed), about 1900. H. 30.0 cm (11 13/16 in). 82.2.20. Formerly in the collections of Mr. and Mrs. Albert C. Revi and Dr. and Mrs. Leonard S. Rakow. Gift of Dr. and Mrs. Rakow.

47. *Andromache.* Amblecote, Thomas Webb & Sons, carved by George Woodall (signed), 1902. H. 31.2 cm (12 1/4 in). 89.2.9. Formerly in the collection of Dr. and Mrs. Leonard S. Rakow. Gift of Mrs. Rakow in memory of Dr. Rakow.

48. Lamp base. Amblecote, Thomas Webb & Sons, probably carved by the Woodall Team, about 1889. H. 45.9 cm (18 1/8 in). 82.2.16. Gift of Dr. and Mrs. Leonard S. Rakow.

49. The showroom of Thomas Goode & Co., London. Photograph, about 1891. Royal Commission on the Historical Monuments of England—Crown Copyright.

50. *The Dancing Girl.* Amblecote, Thomas Webb & Sons, carved by George Woodall (signed), about 1885–1910. H. 30.2 cm (11 7/8 in). 80.2.4. Gift of Dr. and Mrs. Leonard S. Rakow.

51. *Antarctic.* Amblecote, Thomas Webb & Sons, carved by George Woodall, about 1909–1910. H. 35.5 cm (14 in). The Chrysler Museum, Norfolk, Virginia, gift of Walter P. Chrysler, Jr. Reproduced by courtesy of The Chrysler Museum.

52. *Aphrodite and Attendants.* Wordsley, carved by John Northwood II, 1888–1889 and about 1902–1906. D. 38.7 cm (15 1/4 in). 93.2.1. Formerly in the collections of Kenneth Northwood and Dr. and Mrs. Leonard S. Rakow. Gift of Leo, Ruth, and Alan Kaplan, and Susan Kaplan Jacobson.

1. Quoted by Charles R. Hajdamach, *British Glass, 1800–1914*, Woodbridge: Antique Collectors' Club, 1991, p. 82.

2. Michael Braby, "Rivalling the Romans," *Art & Antiques*, September 6, 1975, p. 26.

3. Quoted by Geoffrey W. Beard, *Nineteenth Century Cameo Glass*, Newport, Monmouthshire: The Ceramic Book Co., 1956, p. 6.

4. *Ibid.*, p. 7.

5. *Ibid.*, p. 15.

6. Printed report on the meeting of the Royal Institution on February 12, 1847, preserved in the archives of the institution. I am indebted to Mr. John Smith for this information.

7. Quoted by H. Jack Haden, *Artists in Cameo Glass, Incorporating Thomas Woodall's Memoirs*, Kingswinford: The Black Country Society, 1993, p. 43.

8. Interview with Edwin Grice, *Stourbridge County Express*, March 1, 1913, p. 2.

9. J. M. O'Fallon, "Glass Carving as an Art," *Art Journal*, December 1885, pp. 379–380.

10. Paul V. Gardner, *The Glass of Frederick Carder*, New York: Crown Publishers, 1971, p. 7.

11. Quoted by Paul V. Gardner, *Frederick Carder: Portrait of a Glassmaker* (exhibition catalog), Corning: The Corning Museum of Glass and The Rockwell Museum, 1985, p. 14.